PAPER AIRPLANE BOOK FOR KIDS

Table of Contents

Introduction

Making and flying paper airplanes presents irresistible fun AND being able to make great paper airplanes also gives you bragging rights over other kids, especially when you can build better planes than anyone else!

In this book, you will find plenty of paper airplane designs that will keep you entertained for days on end. The paper airplane designs begin with very easy ones and progress to advanced and expert level designs, so you'll be able to make the coolest planes around. The paper airplanes covered in this book are great for both indoor and outdoor flight. This book also covers the basic principles of flight, so you will learn about aerodynamics and the forces that make flying possible while you're having fun.

Once you learn how to build paper airplanes, every piece of paper lying around the house can be transformed into a flying machine. Are you ready to become the pilot in charge of a squadron of paper airplanes? Let's get started!

Chapter One: Introduction To Paper Airplanes

Paper airplanes are basically pieces of paper that are designed to look and fly like real planes. Sometimes, the art of making paper planes is referred to as *aerogami*, owing to its similarity to origami, the Japanese art of creating models of objects (usually animals) from folded pieces of paper.

Making and flying paper airplanes can be tons of fun! You can play with paper airplanes by yourself or engage in paper airplane competitions with other kids.

Perhaps best of all, knowing how to make paper airplanes can help you learn about how real airplanes fly!

How Do Paper Airplanes Fly?

Just like real planes, paper airplanes rely on the principles of aerodynamics to fly. However, the major difference between the flights of real planes and paper airplanes is that real planes need special designs on their wings to make it possible for them to fly despite their weight. The wings of real planes are usually curved on the top side. This shape makes the distance across the top of the wing longer than the distance across the bottom of the wing, meaning that wind moves faster over the top of the wing than it does below the wing. This creates lower air pressure on the top of wing, pushing the wing and the whole plane upwards, making it possible for the plane to fly despite its weight. Since paper airplanes are made from paper, they are very light and do not need this wing design to be able to fly.

Just like real planes, the ability of a paper airplane to fly depends on four forces. A force is something that pulls or pushes on an object. The four forces that affect the flight of a paper airplane are:

- **Thrust**: This is the force that pushes the paper plane forward through the air.

- **Drag**: This is a force that results from the air pushing against the forward motion of the paper airplane. Drag acts in an opposite direction to thrust.

- **Weight**: This is a force of gravity which pulls down the paper airplane.

- **Lift**: This is a force that keeps the paper plane in the air. Lift acts in an opposite direction to the force of gravity.

When you throw your paper airplane into the air, you are providing it with thrust. The more thrust you provide, the farther and faster your plane will fly, if all other design factors remain unchanged. Once the plane is in the air, the movement of air above and below the wings provides lift, which is the upward force that keeps the plane in the air. Different wing designs result in different amounts of lift for your paper airplane. As the paper airplane moves through the air, the air also tries to oppose this motion, creating a drag force that slows down the plane. The smaller the amount of drag your paper airplane creates, the farther and faster your plane will fly, if all other design factors remain unchanged. Most paper airplane designs try to minimize the amount of drag created by the plane by having a small cross-sectional footprint. The cross-sectional footprint is the size of the plane when observed from the front or back.

Finally, the flight of your paper airplane is affected by its weight. While weight does not affect paper airplanes as much as it affects real planes, it is still an important thing to consider. Lighter planes are more likely to remain in flight for a longer time, so you need to keep your paper airplane as light as possible.

History Of Paper Airplanes

People were making paper airplanes long before the first real plane was invented. The history of paper airplanes can be traced back to ancient China, where, over 2000 years ago, the Chinese used papyrus paper to create flying paper kites and gliders. Since the Chinese are credited with having created paper, it comes as no surprise that they were the first ones to find creative uses of paper besides its use in writing. Unfortunately, owing to the delicate nature of paper, none of the paper gliders made by the ancient Chinese has survived to date. In Europe, people started experimenting with paper airplanes during the Renaissance period. In the late 1400s, Leonardo da Vinci is recorded as having used parchment to create models of his flying machine, which was known as an ornithopter. In the 1700s, an interesting use of paper for flight was recorded when the Montgovier brothers built hot air balloons using paper. In 1783, the brothers used paper-lined cloth to build the first hot air balloons capable of carrying humans.

In the early 1900s, as people became more obsessed with achieving flight, many inventors and researchers used paper airplane models to understand the effect of aerodynamic principles. The Wright brothers, who are credited with having invented the modern airplane as we know it, used paper airplanes in wind tunnels to test out their plane designs. In the 1930s, the Lockheed Corporation tested various designs using paper models before implementing the designs in production aircraft.

When World War II started, the usage of several materials was restricted by governments in order to preserve the materials for war uses. This reduced the availability of materials such as metal, plastic, and wood for making toys. Paper, which was widely available and did not have much use in the war, became the go-to material for toy-making. People started using paper to make models of the fighter planes that were being used in the war. Once the war ended and the restrictions on materials were lifted, the use of paper in toy-making declined, though it did not die off completely. Today, the ability to make paper airplanes is a skill that kids take pride in, and flying paper airplanes is an activity that many children across the world enjoy.

Chapter Two: Beginner Paper Airplane Designs

In this chapter, we will look at paper airplane designs that are relatively easy to build, even for someone who has no prior experience building paper airplanes.

The Basic

This is a very basic paper airplane that is one of the first ones most people learn how to build. Building this plane is very easy and does not require lots of time. It also flies fairly well and can remain in the air for a while.

Folding Instructions

1. Take a piece of paper and fold it along the center as shown in Step 1 and then unfold it, creating a crease.

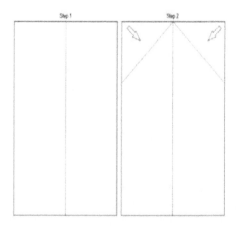

2. Fold the top corners of the piece of paper until they touch crease you made in the middle of the paper, as shown in Step 2.

3. Fold the piece of paper in half along the crease so that you end up with the shape shown in Step 3.

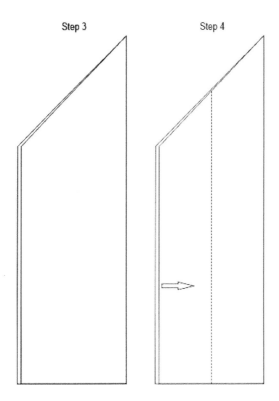

4. You will have two flaps now facing the left. Fold each flap in half as shown in Step 4 to create the wings of your paper airplane.

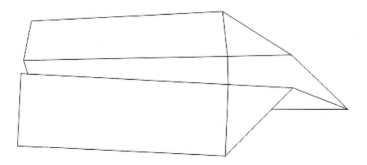

5. Congratulations! You just made your first paper airplane. Toss it into the air and enjoy your new career as a paper airplane pilot!

Basic Dart

This is another simple and popular paper airplane design that will achieve good speeds and cover a great distance. Like the previous design, the Basic Dart is very easy to build in a short time. You can have your Basic Dart ready to fly in less than a minute.

Folding Instructions

1. Start with a plain piece of paper and fold it in half and then unfold it. The aim is to create a crease running from top to bottom, as shown in Step 1.

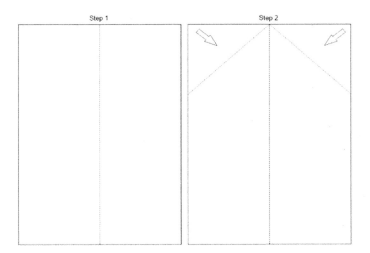

2. Fold the top corners of your paper until they touch the crease you just created, as shown in Step 2.

3. Fold the two flaps again, this time diagonally, as shown in Step 3. Your piece of paper should look like the image on the right when you are finished.

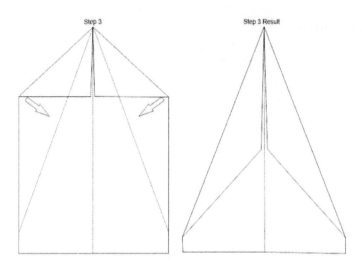

4. Fold the paper in half by bringing together the two outer edges so that your plane now looks like the image below.

5. Fold each side so that the top edge meets the bottom edge. This process will create wings for your plane. Your paper airplane is now complete. When observed from above, it should look as shown below.

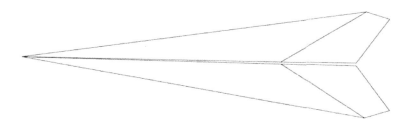

The Stable

This plane is a bit more complex compared to the previous two. However, it, as its name suggests, is very stable and if you build it properly, you can achieve lots of distance with this plane. You can even get the plane to perform some exciting stunts by slightly bending the rear sections of the wings upwards. Doing this also reduces the chances of the plane stalling after you throw it into the air.

Folding Instructions

1. As you're probably used to by now, start by folding a plain piece of paper in half and then unfold to create a crease, as shown in Step 1.

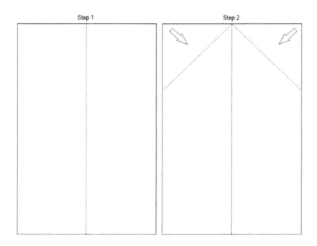

2. Fold down the top corners until they touch the crease you just created, as shown in Step 2.

3. The top of your paper now looks like a triangle. Fold the triangle down, towards the center of the paper, so that the paper almost looks like a square. It should resemble the image shown on the next page.

4. Fold the top corners diagonally towards the center, but do not let them meet at the crease. Leave a small space between the corners and the center crease, about a centimeter long. Your paper should now look like the image shown below.

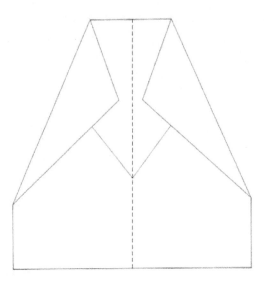

5. Fold up the triangle at the center so that it holds the two side flaps in place as shown below.

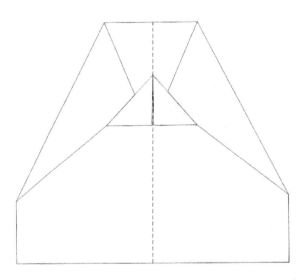

6. Fold the entire plane in half along the center crease. Your plane should now look like the image on the next page.

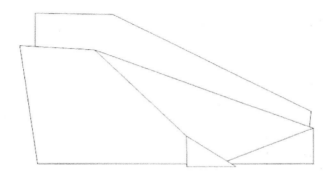

7. Finally, fold down the top edges of the paper to create the wings. Make your fold about half an inch from the bottom of the plane. Your plane should resemble the one shown below. You are now ready to launch your plane into the air!

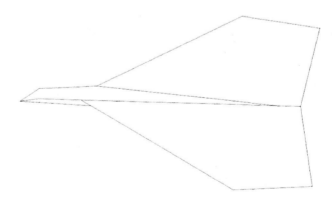

The Shadow

The shadow is an easy to make paper plane that also looks cool. It is a fun plane that you will enjoy building. It also flies very well.

Folding Instructions

1. Start by placing a rectangular piece of paper in landscape mode. Fold it in half along a centerline running vertically across the paper, then unfold so that you have a crease as shown in the image below.

2. Fold the right half of the paper along a diagonal line running from the top of the crease to the bottom right corner as shown in the image below.

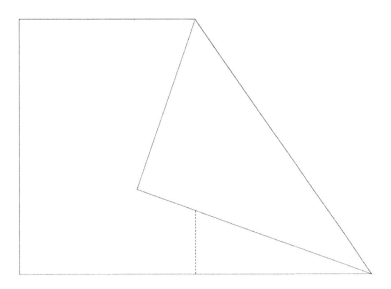

3. Repeat step two with the left side, so that your paper now looks as shown below.

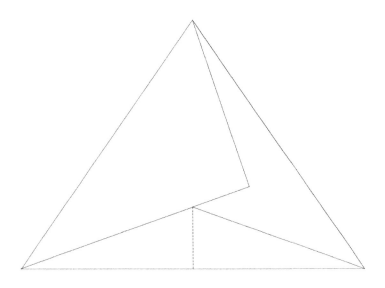

4. Fold the paper in half along the centerline crease so that the paper now looks as shown in the image below.

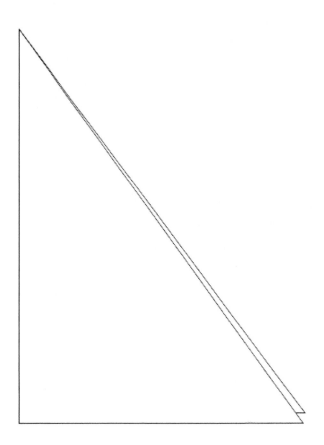

5. Rotate the plane so that the sharp apex points to your left. Fold the top flap so that it aligns with the bottom edge of the plane as shown below. This will form a wing for your plane.

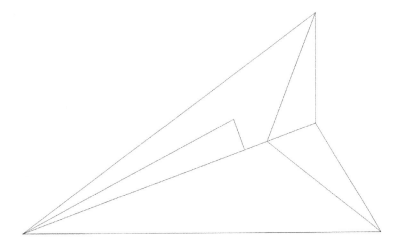

6. Repeat step five with the other flap, taking care to leave the small triangular flap at the center of the plane sticking out. Your plane should now look like the image below.

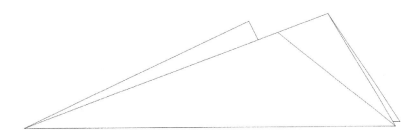

7. Fold the edges of the wings upwards as shown below to form stabilizers for your plane.

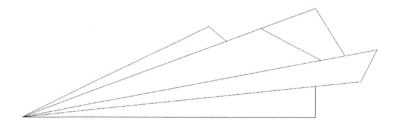

8. Open up the wings in readiness for flight. Your plane should now look like the image below.

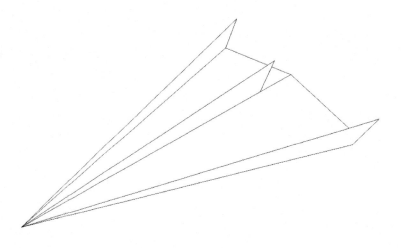

Lock Bottom Plane

This is another plane that is fairly easy to make. The greatest feature of the Lock Bottom Plane is the great distances it is capable of reaching. The best part is that you don't even have to throw it very hard, making it ideal even for younger kids.

Folding Instructions

1. Fold a piece of paper in half and then unfold to create a crease along the center, as shown in Step 1.

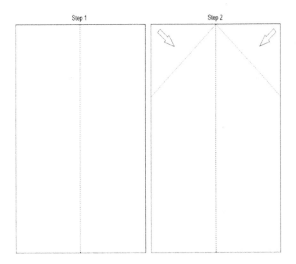

2. Fold the top corners towards the center so that they meet at the crease, as shown in Step 2 above.

3. Fold the triangle created at the top of the paper down so that your paper looks like an envelope, as shown on the next page.

Leave a space of about ¾ of an inch between the tip of the triangle and the bottom edge.

4. Fold the two top corners diagonally towards the center, as shown below.

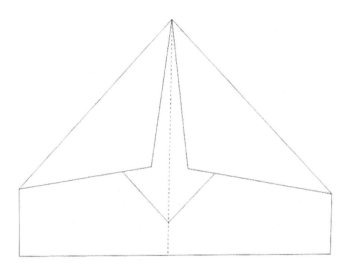

5. Fold up the tip of the triangle so that it holds the two flaps in place, as shown on the next page.

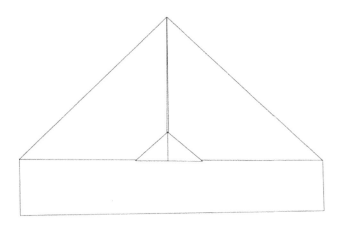

6. Fold your plane in half along the original crease you made. Your plane should now look like the image below.

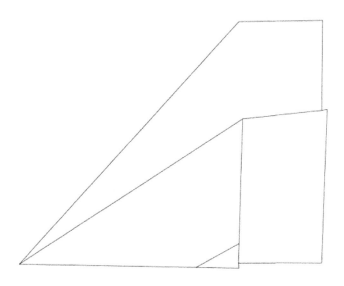

7. Fold the side flaps towards the bottom of the plane to create wings for your plane. Then, fold the end of each wing upwards, about half an inch from the tip of the wing.

8. Finally, cut two slits at the rear end of each wing and fold the section of paper between them upwards. Your plane is now complete. It should look like the image below.

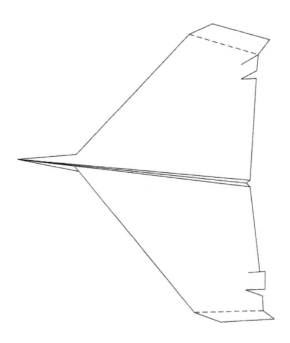

Tailspin

The Tailspin is another easy-to-build paper airplane that has a unique tail design. All the planes you've made so far typically fly in a straight path and land smoothly. The Tailspin, on the other hand, spirals through the air and lands in a tailspin, hence the name!

Folding Instructions

1. Start by folding your piece of paper by half and then unfolding the paper so that a crease running from top to bottom remains, as shown in Step 1.

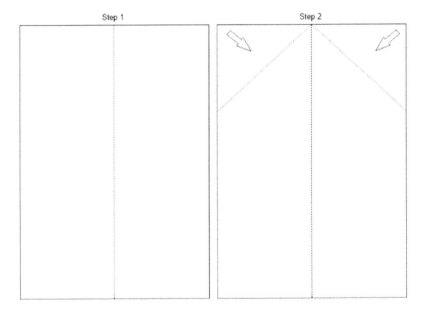

2. Fold the two top corners of your paper towards the crease at the center, as shown in Step 2.

3. Fold the new top corners towards the center so that they meet in the middle and the piece of paper looks like the image shown on the next page.

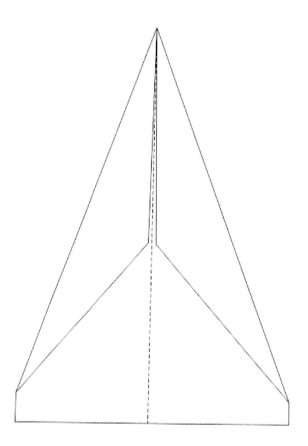

4. About an inch from the top, fold down the tip of your plane. Your plane should now look like the image shown on the next page.

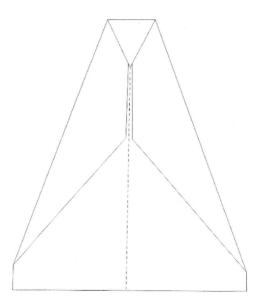

5. Now fold your plane in half along the crease running down the center so that it resembles the image below.

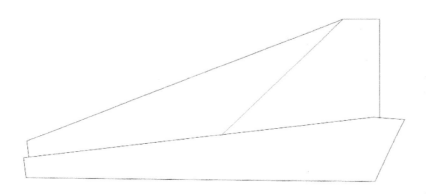

6. Fold down the side flaps towards the bottom edge to create wings for your plane. Line up the edge of each wing with the

bottom edge of the plane to make sure they are even. Your plane should now look like the image below.

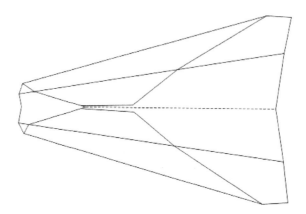

7. Finally, fold the rear tip of one wing upwards and the other one downwards to create the special tail design. Your completed plane should look like the image below. You can now enjoy watching your plane spiral through the air!

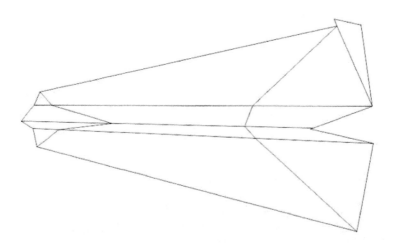

The Arrow

The Arrow is a plane that is designed for speed. Building the Arrow is very easy and can be done in less than a minute. The Arrow's design included "elevators," which help you control the angle at which your plane will fly!

Folding Instructions

1. Fold a piece of paper by half vertically. Then unfold the paper so that a crease remains at the center of the paper, as shown in Step 1.

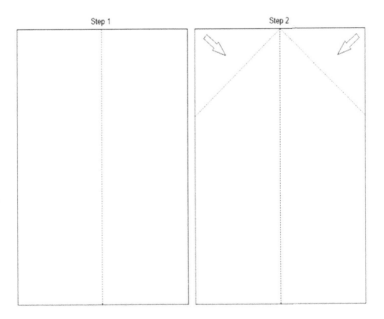

2. Fold the two top corners towards the crease at the center, as shown in Step 2. They should meet at the crease.

3. Fold down the new top corners of the paper so that they meet at the center crease and you get the shape shown in Step 3 on the next page.

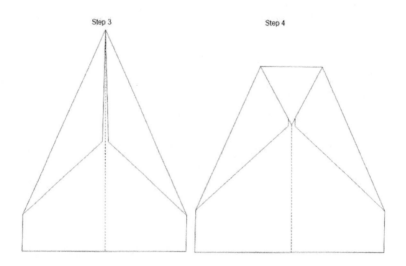

4. Fold down the tip of your plane so that it hits where the other two tips meet, as shown in Step 4.

5. Flip over your plane and then fold it in half along the center crease. This will result in the shape shown in Step 5.

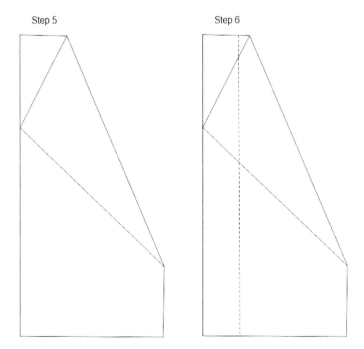

Step 5   Step 6

6. Fold down the side flaps along the dotted line shown in Step 6 to create wings for your plane.

7. Finally, using a pair of scissors, cut two slits into the tail end of each of your plane's wings, about an inch apart. Lift up the section of paper between the two slits to act as elevator adjustments for your plane. Try experimenting with how the different positions of the elevators affect your plane's flight path!

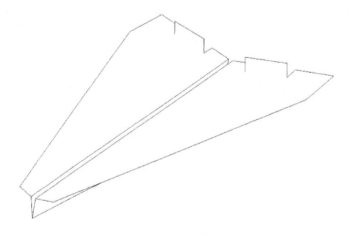

Additionally, you can tilt your plane's wings up slightly so that the plan looks like a letter "Y" when observed from the back. Doing this will make your plane's flight smoother and faster.

The Royal Glider

This is a paper plane that is fairly easy to build and will be ready for take-off in under a minute. The Royal Glider is built for distance and flight time.

Folding Instructions

1. Start by folding your piece of paper in half horizontally. Then, unfold the paper so that a horizontal crease remains, as shown below.

2. Fold down the top edge so that it aligns with the centerline crease, as shown below.

3. Once again, fold down the top part of the paper with the centerline crease as the reference, as shown in the image below.

4. Fold down the top corners so that they meet the horizontal line at the center, as shown below.

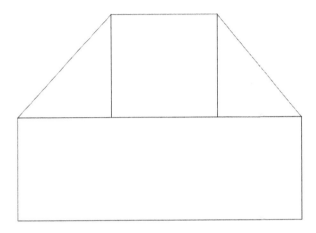

5. Fold down the top edge so that it touches the line at the center, as shown below.

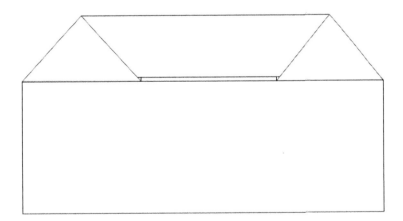

6. Turn over the paper and fold it in half horizontally, so that it ends up looking like the image below.

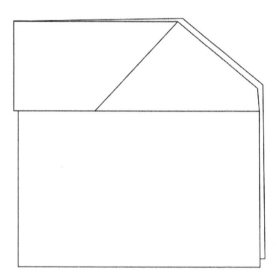

7. Fold the top flap about half an inch from the left edge to create a wing for your plane. The plane should now look like the image below.

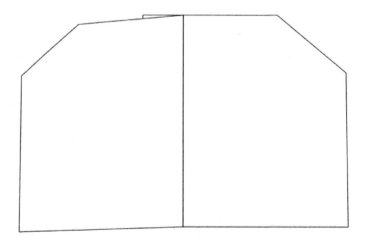

8. Repeat the previous step with the other flap to create the other wing for your plane so that your plane now looks as shown below.

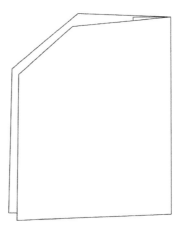

9. Fold the tips of the wings about half an inch from the top to create stabilizers for your plane, as shown below.

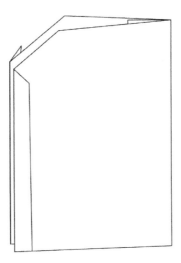

10. Open up the wings. The complete Royal Glider should look like the image below.

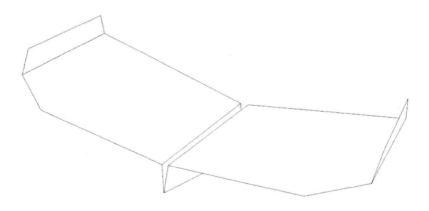

Chapter Three: Intermediate Paper Airplane Designs

In this chapter, we take a look at paper airplane designs that can be slightly more advanced than the designs we looked at in the previous chapter, though they are still relatively easy to build. The designs covered in this section are the perfect way to build your confidence before moving on to more advanced designs.

The Canard

The canard is a fairly easy to make plane with a very unique design. This plane is very stable in flight and will give you amazing flight time.

Folding Instructions

1. Start by folding your piece of paper in half vertically. Unfold it so that a crease remains, as shown below.

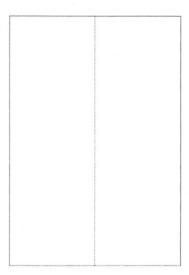

2. Fold the paper down so that about a third of the paper remains at the bottom, as shown below.

3. Fold the top right corner diagonally towards the inner part of the paper, as shown below.

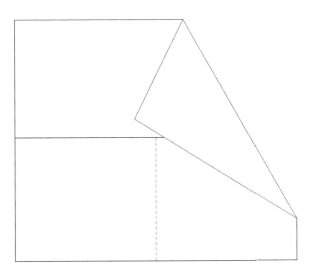

4. Repeat Step 3 with the top left corner, as shown below.

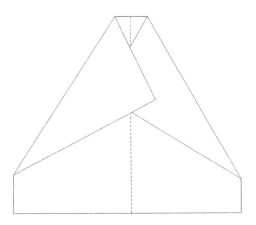

5. Fold the corners of the flaps you just created outwards, as shown on the next page.

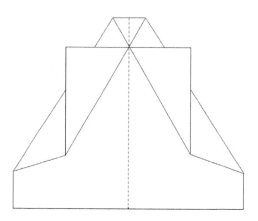

6. Fold the plane in half along the centerline crease, so that your plane looks like the image below.

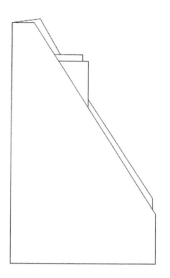

7. Fold the top of the outside flap about half an inch from the bottom edge to create a wing for your plane. Your plane should now look like the image below.

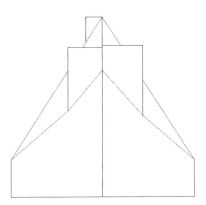

8. Fold the other flap to create a second wing for your plane, so that your plane now looks as shown below.

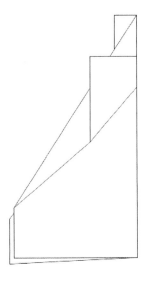

9. Open up the wings of your plane. The complete Canard should look like the image shown below.

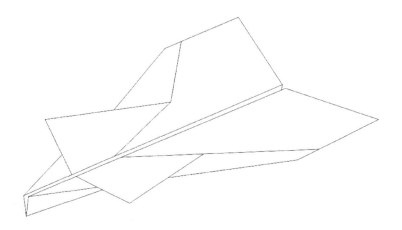

Lift Off

This is a plane that is designed for distance. It launches with a lot of power and is the perfect plane to win distance competitions against other paper airplane pilots.

Folding Instructions

1. Like most of the planes we have built so far, start this one by folding your piece of paper in half and then unfolding the paper to create a vertical crease, as shown in Step 1.

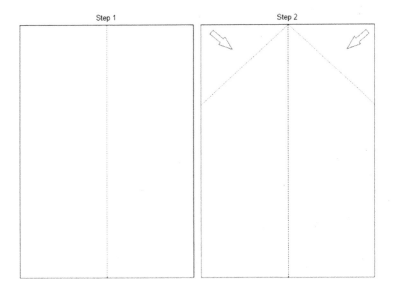

2. Fold the top corners towards the center so that they meet at the crease, as shown in Step 2.

3. About an inch from the top, fold the top tip of the plane backwards. This will create a shape like the one shown in Step 3 on the next page.

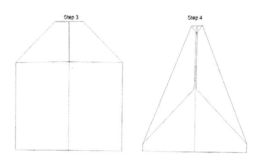

4. Fold the top edges in towards the center crease, as shown in Step 4 above.

5. Fold your plane in half along the center crease, as shown in Step 5 below.

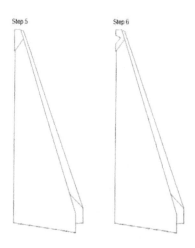

6. Using a pair of scissors, cut out a small triangle from your plane tip, as shown in Step 6.

7. Fold down the side flaps towards the bottom edge to create wings for your plane. Your plane should now look like the image shown below. Notice that the plane will have a hole near its nose.

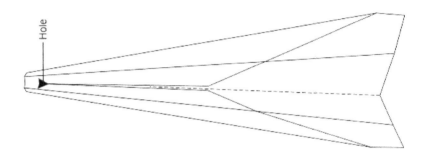

8. Secure a rubber band around the notch at the plane's nose (shown below) and use it to launch your plane forcefully across the room. If you feel that the nose is not strong enough, you can reinforce it using a piece of tape to prevent it from tearing as you pull on the rubber band.

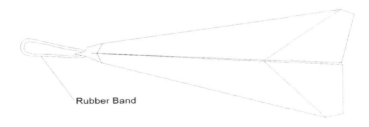

The Buzz

This is one of the easiest planes to build in this chapter. The Buzz gets its name from the fact that is looks like a fly. This plane will give you great distances and a lot of flight time.

Folding Instructions

1. Unlike the paper airplanes we have made so far, we will use a square piece of paper for this plane instead of a rectangular one. Take the square piece of paper and fold it in half vertically and then unfold it to create a crease, as shown below.

2. Fold down the two top corners of the piece of paper so that they meet at the crease you created, as shown on the next page.

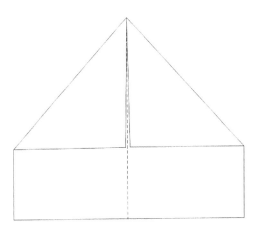

3. Fold down the triangle created at the top of the paper so that its tip lines up with the bottom edges of the flaps you created. Your piece of paper should now resemble the image below.

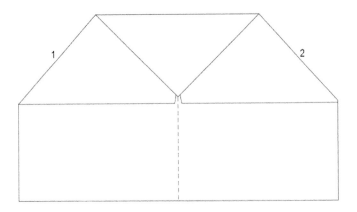

4. Fold in the diagonal edges marked 1 and 2 in the previous image so that they meet at the crease at the center of the paper. The image below shows what it should look like when you lift the flaps you've just made.

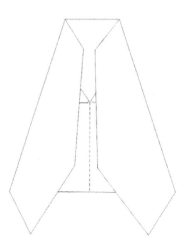

5. About half an inch from the top, fold backwards.

6. Fold the plane in half along the center crease. At this point, your plane should look like the image shown below.

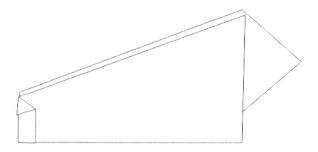

7. Fold down the side flaps to create wings for your plane. Make the fold for your wings about half an inch from the bottom edge of the plane. If you are having trouble keeping the wings together in the middle, you can use a piece of tape to hold them, as shown below. Your plane is now complete!

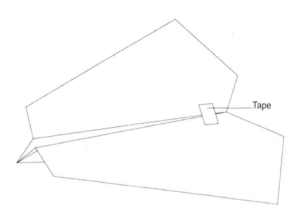

Additionally, you can bend the tail ends of your plane's wings to control its flight. If you want it to perform stunts and acrobatic maneuvers, bend the tail end of one wing upwards and the other one downwards.

The V-Wing

This is another easy to make paper plane that flies smoothly and noiselessly like a spy plane. The V-Wing will give you lots of distance and flight time.

Folding Instructions

1. Just like the Buzz, the V-Wing requires a square piece of paper instead of a rectangular one. Take the square piece of paper and fold it in half vertically and then unfold it to create a crease, as shown below.

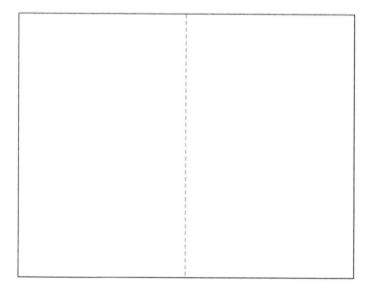

2. Fold down the two top corners of the piece of paper so that they meet at the crease you created, as shown below.

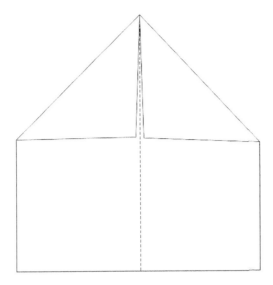

3. Fold the top apex so that it touches the point where the two flaps meet, as shown below.

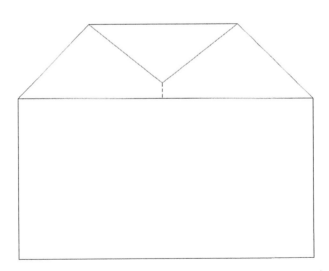

4. Once again, fold the upper corners of the paper towards the centerline crease as shown below.

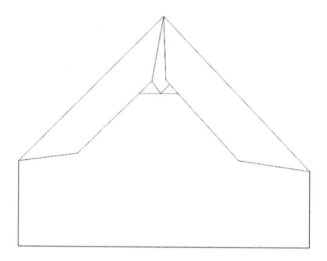

5. Fold the plane in half along the centerline crease so that it now looks as shown on the next page.

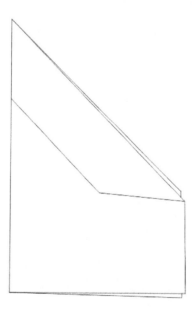

6. Fold the upper flap of the plane to form the wing as shown below.

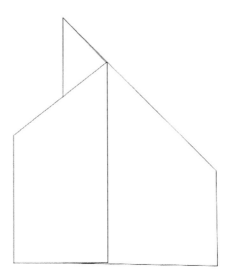

7. Repeat the previous step with the other flap to create the second wing.

8. Unfold the wings. The complete V-Wing should look like the image below.

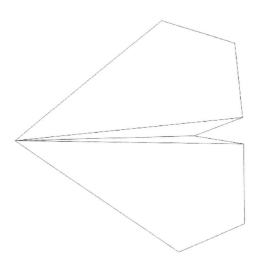

The Sprinter

The Sprinter is a plane that is designed to look like a jet, though it does not fly like a jet. Depending on how you launch the Sprinter, its wings might flap, affecting its flight. The best way to launch the sprinter is to gently throw it. The Sprinter is best known for its distance and acrobatics.

Folding Instructions

1. Starting with a rectangular piece of paper, fold the paper so that the top left corner touches the bottom right corner, as shown in the image below.

2. Fold over the long diagonal edge by about ¾ of an inch, as shown on the next page.

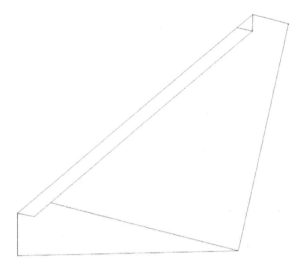

3. Fold the paper in half diagonally towards you so that the top right corner meets the bottom left corner. Then, rotate the paper so that the two edges with the extra piece folded over face the top and left. Your paper should resemble the one shown below.

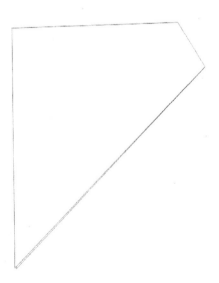

4. Fold only the top flap diagonally in half, as shown in the image below.

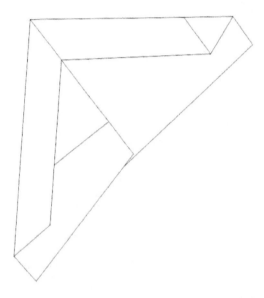

5. Fold down the other flap in the opposite direction. By now, your plane should look as shown on the next page.

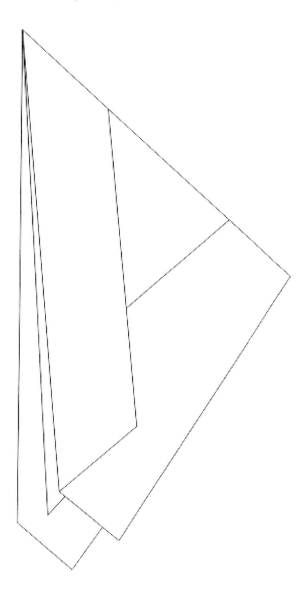

6. Fold down the top flap to form one wing. This fold should be about ¾ of an inch from the bottom of the plane.

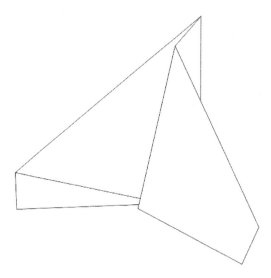

7. Fold down the bottom flap to form the other wing, as shown below.

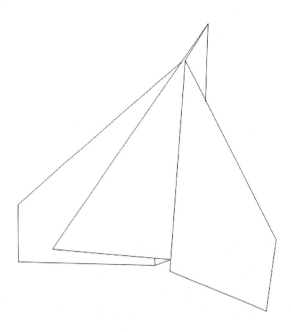

8. Your Sprinter is now complete. Your final design should look like the image below.

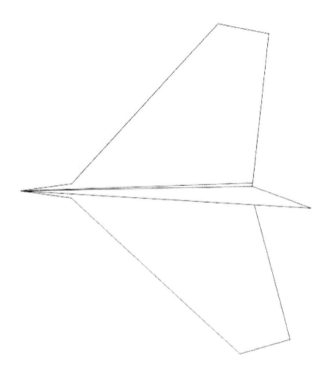

The Sea Glider

The Sea Glider gets its name from the fact that its shape makes it look like a seagull gliding over the ocean. This paper airplane allows you to get creative. By bending the wings in different ways, you can alter its flight. The Sea Glider is built for distance and remains in the air for quite some time.

Folding Instructions

1. Fold the piece of paper diagonally so that the top right corner touches the left edge, as shown in the image below.

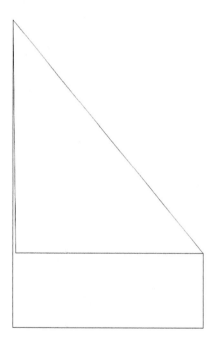

2. Using a pair of scissors, trim off the paper remaining uncovered at the bottom so that you are left with a triangle shape, as shown on the next page.

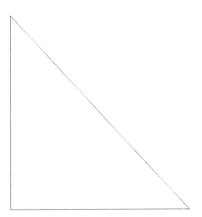

3. Fold the long diagonal side over about 1½ inches from the edge, as shown below.

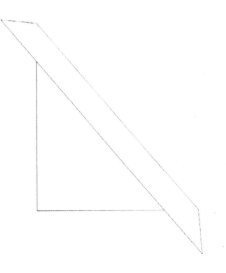

4. Fold your plane in half diagonally from top left to bottom right. The ends of the piece you folded over should touch and match up. Once you have done this, rotate your paper so that the long edge is at the top, as shown in the image below.

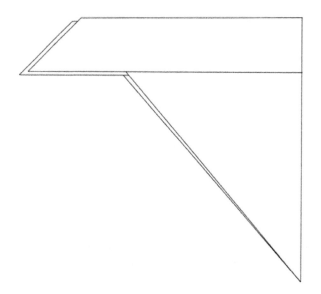

5. Fold the two top edges (with the long piece) diagonally outwards so that they are folded down but still match up. This should create the shape shown below.

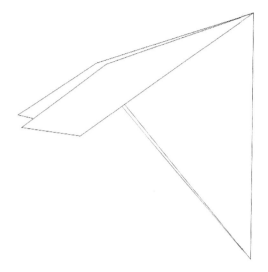

6. Fold over one flap to create a wing. Make this fold about ¾ of an inch from the bottom edge of the plane. The folded flap can be seen on the right side of the image below.

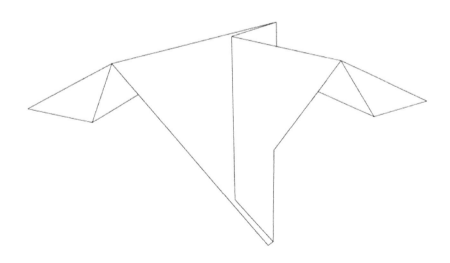

7. Fold over the other flap to create the other wing. Your Sea
   Glider is now complete! From above, your plane should look
   like the image shown below.

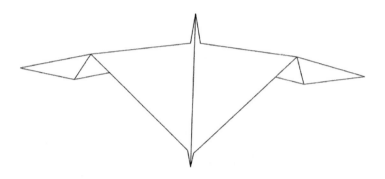

The Hunting Plane

The Hunting Plane is designed for distance and flight time. The design gives the plane a heavy nose, which helps it overcome drag and maintain its momentum over a long distance, especially if you throw it hard enough. In addition, the wide wings provide it with enough lift to remain airborne for an impressively long time.

Folding Instructions

1. Start by folding your piece of paper in half vertically, and then unfolding it so that you create a crease along the center of the paper, as shown below.

2. About 2 inches from the edge, fold the top of the paper down, as shown on the next page.

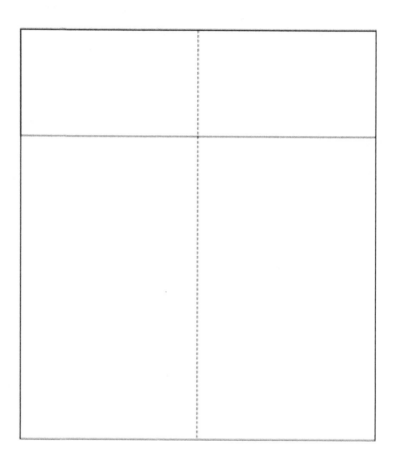

3. Fold the flap you've made down from the top again, this time in half. This will double and thicken the top part, as shown below.

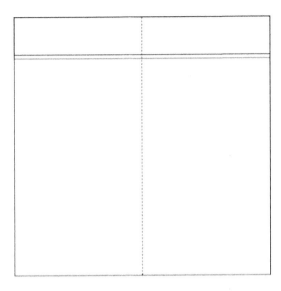

4. Fold the top part in half once again, as shown below.

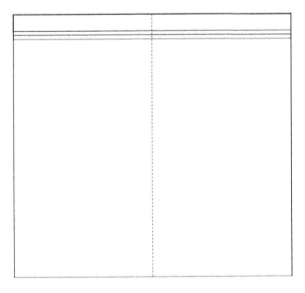

5. Fold the top corners of the paper backwards so that they meet behind the center crease. Your paper should now look like the image below.

6. Fold the plane in half along the vertical crease. This will create a plane similar to the image shown below.

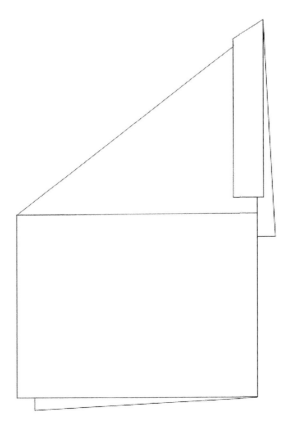

7. Fold down the side flaps to create the wings for your plane. Remember that the thick point is the nose of your plane and so the flaps are folded down toward it. The folds should be made about half an inch above the bottom edge and at a slight angle.

8. Finally, fold the edges of the wings upwards, about half an inch from the edge. Doing this makes your paper airplane faster. Your complete hunter plane should resemble the image on the next page.

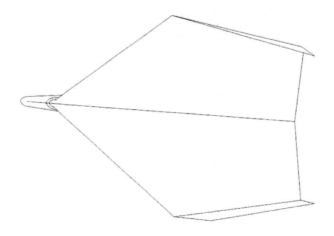

Chapter Four: Advanced Paper Airplane Designs

In this chapter, we look at paper airplane designs that are a bit more complicated than the planes in Chapter Three. The designs covered in this chapter are the perfect way to show off your paper airplane-making skills to your friends and family.

The Wildcat Fighter Paper Jet

The Wildcat Fighter is modeled after one of the most famous fighter jets of World War II. As you might expect of a plane that is built for war, the Wildcat Fighter will achieve great speeds.

Folding Instructions

1. Start by folding a rectangular piece of paper in half vertically. Unfold the paper so that you have a crease, as shown in Step 1 below.

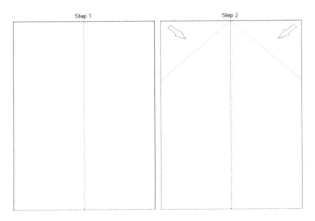

2. Fold the two top corners of the paper so that they meet at the center crease, as shown in Step 2 above.

3. Fold down the diagonal edges of the paper by about half an inch from the edge so that the paper looks like the image on the next page.

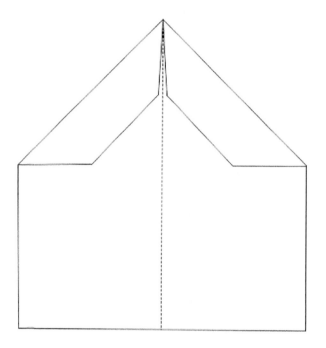

4. Fold down the top triangular section of the paper, leaving a space of about half an inch between the point of the triangle and the bottom edge of the paper, as shown below.

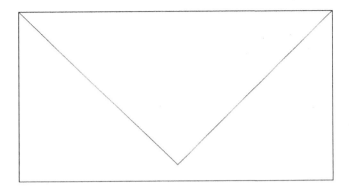

5. Fold the triangular flap upwards. This fold should be about 1½ inches from the top edge of the paper. Your plane should now look like the image on the next page.

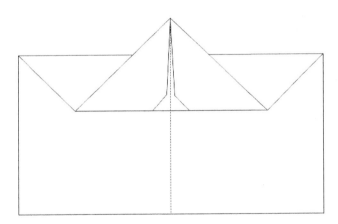

6. Flip your plane over and fold it in half vertically so that it looks like the image shown below.

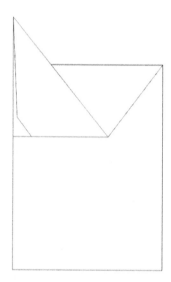

7. Fold the top flap about an inch from the left edge to create a wing for your plane. Flip the plane over and fold down the other flap to create the other wing. After this step, your plane should resemble the image below.

8. About one centimeter from the edge of the wings, fold the edges of the wings upwards to create fins.

9. Unfold the wings (with the fins folded in) so that the plane looks like it did in Step 6. Using a pair of scissors, cut out the wings of your plane as shown below.

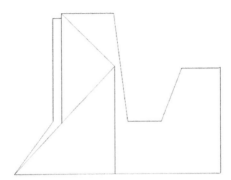

10. Finally, fold the wings again along the creases you created in Step 7. Your complete Wildcat Fighter paper jet should now look like the image below.

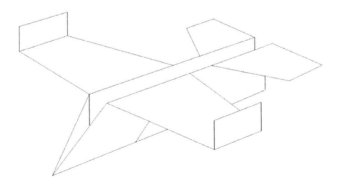

Delta Fighter

The Delta Fighter is a paper airplane that is designed for speed and distance, modeled after the delta-winged fighters of World War II.

Folding Instructions

1. Start by folding a rectangular piece of paper by half vertically and unfolding it so that a crease remains along the center of the paper, as shown in Step 1.

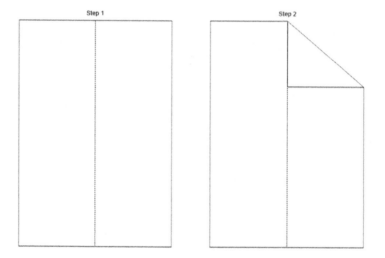

2. Fold the top right corner of the paper so that it touches the centerline crease, as shown in Step 2.

3. Fold the top left corner towards the right edge of the paper, as shown in Step 3.

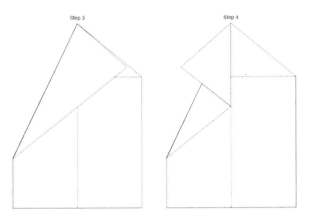

4. Fold this flap back so that the folded edge is aligned with the center crease, as shown in Step 4.

5. Fold the part of the flap extending outside the body of the paper so that its folded edge aligns with the diagonal edge of the paper, as shown in Step 5.

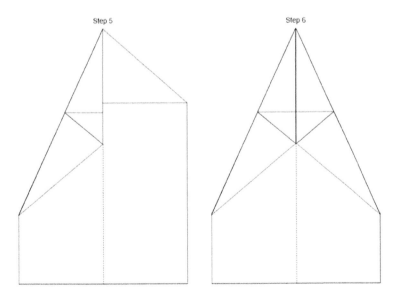

6. Repeat steps 3 through 5 on the right so that your paper looks like the image shown in Step 6.

7. Fold the paper in half along the crease at the center so that all the folds you have made are hidden. Your plane should now look like the image below.

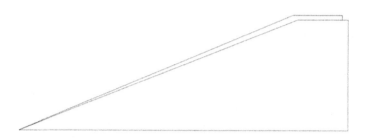

8. Fold down the side flaps along the crease indicated below to create wings for your plane.

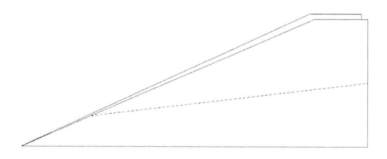

9. Your complete Delta Fighter should have a cockpit sticking out, as shown in the image below.

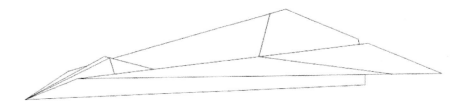

Underside Plane

This paper plane is a very stable plane that will give you plenty of flight time, owing to its extra underside flaps which help keep it aloft.

Folding Instructions

1. Fold your piece of paper in half vertically and then unfold it. Fold the paper in half again, this time horizontally, and then unfold it so that you have two creases across your paper as shown below.

2. Fold down the top of the paper so that it touches the horizontal crease, as shown on the next page.

3. Fold the top edge of the paper downwards along the horizontal crease, as shown below.

4. Fold down the top corners of your piece of paper, as shown on the next page.

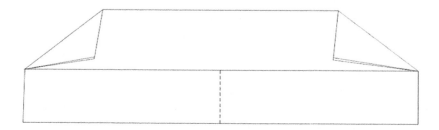

5. Once again, fold the two top corners towards the center, as shown below.

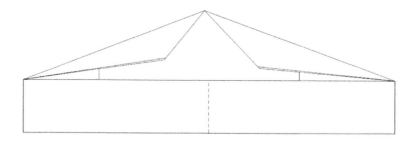

6. Now, fold the top point of your plane downwards, as shown in the image below.

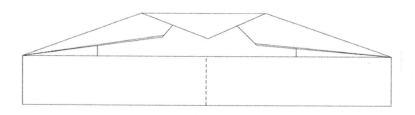

7. Turn your piece of paper over and fold it in half along the vertical centerline. The plane should now look as shown below.

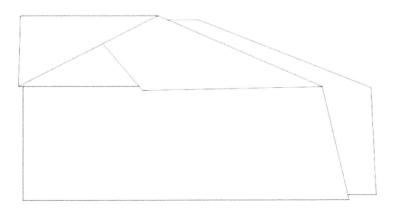

8. Fold the top flap over about an inch from the left edge to create a wing for your plane. Repeat with the other flap to create the other wing. At this point, your plane should resemble the image below.

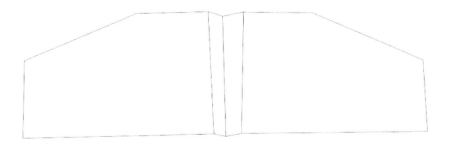

9. Squeeze the wings of your plane together. Your complete underwing plane should look like the image on the next page.

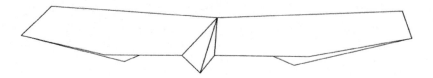

The Spear Plane

This is a plane that is designed to cut through the air like a spear. When launched powerfully enough, the Spear Plane will give you both great speed and great distance.

Folding Instructions

1. Fold the top right corner of your paper until it touches the left edge, with the crease beginning at the bottom right corner, as shown below.

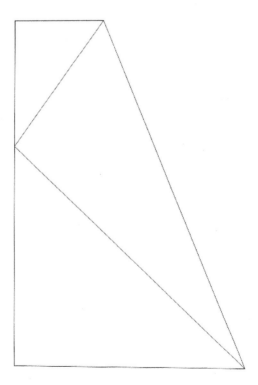

2. Open up the paper so that a crease remains. Repeat the fold with the opposite side, so that the top left corner touches the edge of the paper.

3. Open up the paper and fold the right corner so that it aligns with the first crease you created, as shown in the image on the next page.

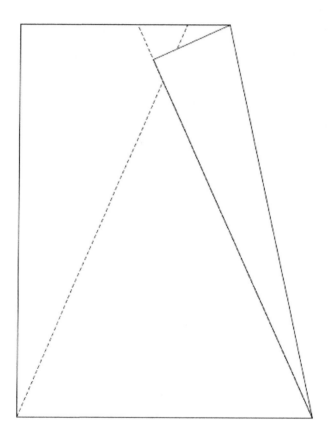

4. Repeat with the other side so that your paper looks like the image on the next page.

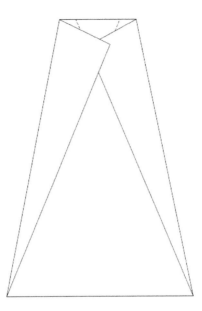

5. Fold the right edge inwards again, aligning it with the tip of the folded left flap. Your paper should now look like the image on the next page.

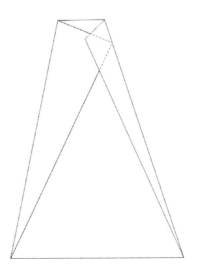

6. Repeat this with the other side so that you end up with the shape shown below.

7. Fold the top edge of your paper down so that it touches the point where the two layers cross each other, as shown below.

8. Flip your paper over and fold it in half vertically. Your paper should resemble the image shown below.

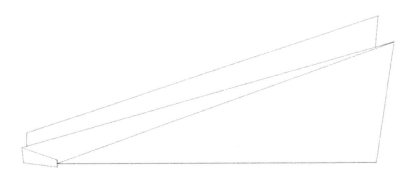

9. Fold down the top flap at an angle to form one wing, and then repeat with the other flap to create the other wing. Your plane should now look like the image below.

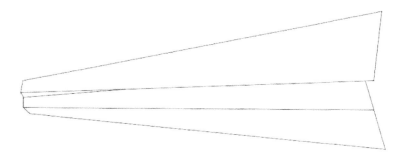

10. Squeeze the wings of your plane together so that your plane looks like the image below.

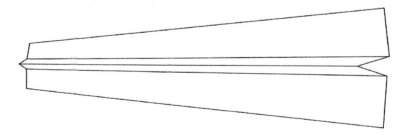

Heavy-Nosed Plane

This plane, when completed, looks like the Basic Dart. However, it has additional folds which make its nose heavier, thus allowing this plane to fly for a longer distance than the basic dart.

Folding Instructions

1. Fold your piece of paper in half vertically. Unfold the paper so that a crease remains, as shown in Step 1.

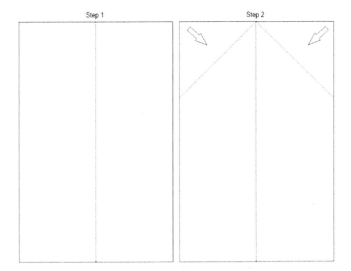

2. Fold the two top corners as shown in Step 2 so that they touch the crease you created in Step 1.

3. Once again, fold the top corners of your paper so that they meet at the center crease, as shown in the image on the next page.

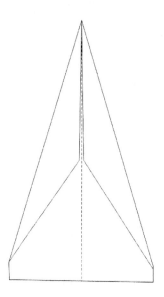

4. Fold down the top point of the plane so that it touches the bottom edge of the plane, as shown below.

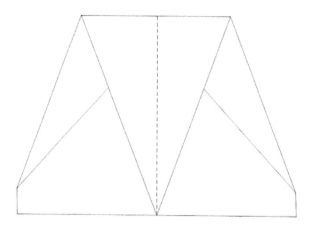

5. Fold this flap upwards about 2½ inches from the top edge. Your plane should now resemble the image below.

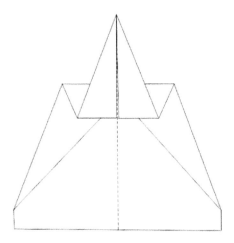

6. Fold the point of your plane downwards about 1½ inches from the tip, as shown below.

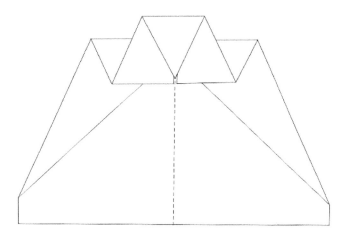

7. Fold the plane in half along the vertical crease and then fold out the wings.

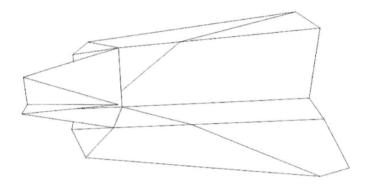

8. Finally, bring together the two wings. Your complete plane should look like the image shown below.

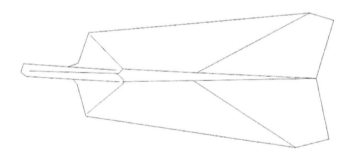

The Uranus Arc

The Uranus Arc is a great paper airplane that looks really cool when completed. However, if you want the Uranus Arc to fly really well, you should ensure you fold it very carefully and all the folds are sharp and straight.

Folding Instructions

1. Start with a rectangular piece of paper and fold it in half vertically. Unfold the paper so that a crease remains along the center of the paper, as shown in Step 1.

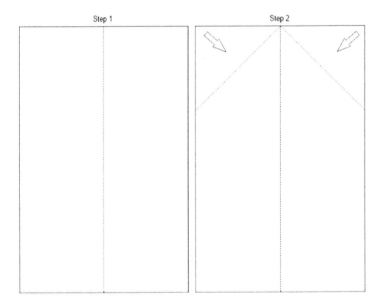

2. Fold the top corners of the paper as shown in Step 2 so that they touch the crease you created in Step 1.

3. Once again, fold the top corners of your paper so that they meet at the center line, as shown in the image on the next page.

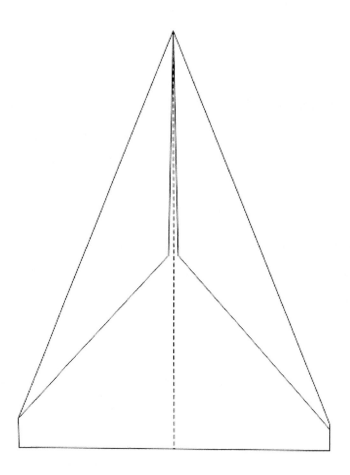

4. Fold down the top point of the plane so that it touches the bottom edge of the plane, as shown below.

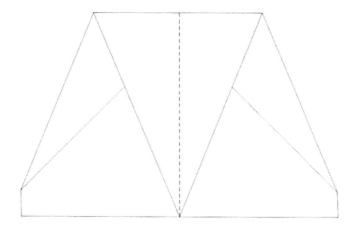

5. Turn your paper over and fold the two top corners so that bottom edges of the flap created are parallel to the bottom edge. Your paper should now look like the image below.

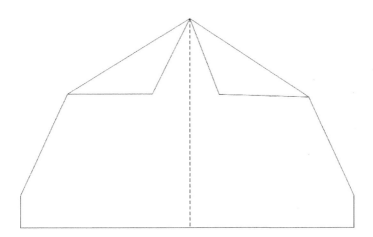

6. Fold the top point downwards over the flaps, and at the same time, lift the flap that you created on the backside upwards. Your paper should now resemble the image below.

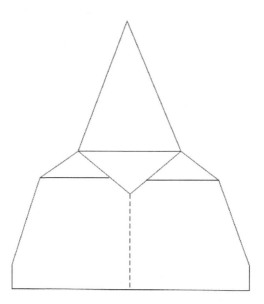

7. Turn your plane over so that it looks like the image below.

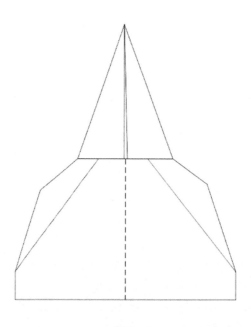

8. Fold your plane in half along the vertical crease so that you now have the shape on the next page.

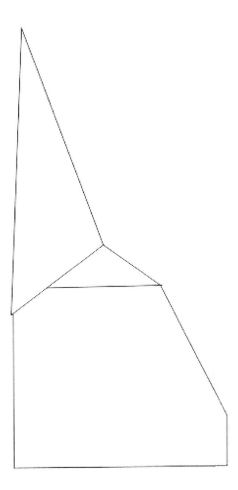

9. Fold down the top flap to create a wing for your plane. Turn the plane over and fold down the other flap to create the other wing, taking care to ensure that both wings are aligned. At this point, your plane should look like the image below.

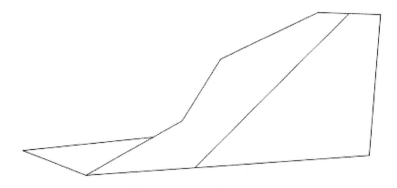

10. Unfold the wings so that your plane resembles the image below.

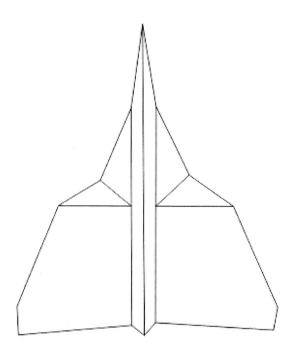

11. Turn your plane over and make a fold on each wing to create fins. The folds should start at the top corner of the wings, while the bottom edges of the fins should be aligned with the bottom edges of the wings, as shown in the image below.

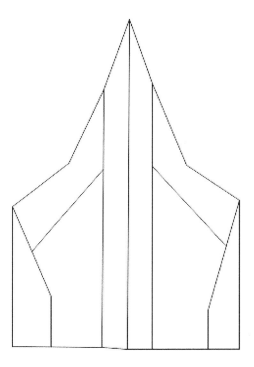

12. Finally, unfold the fins and lift them upwards so that they are facing up vertically. Tilt up the wings slightly so that they form a letter "V" when observed from behind. Doing this will make your plane more stable while flying. Your plane is now ready for flight. The complete Uranus Arc should look like the image below.

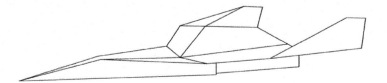

Navy Plane

This paper airplane is modeled after the fighter jets used by the navy. Like the impressive navy fighter jets, this paper airplane will give you impressive speed, distance, and flight time. The navy plane is also one of my favorite paper plane designs, since it is simple to make and looks very cool.

Folding Instructions

1. Place a rectangular piece of paper in landscape mode and then fold it in half vertically. Unfold it so that you are left with a crease, as shown below.

2. Fold down the two top corners so that they touch the center crease, as shown below.

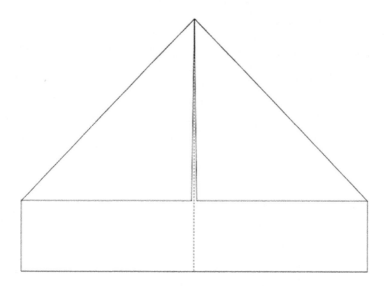

3. Fold down the top point towards the center of the paper where the other two corners meet. The paper should resemble the image below.

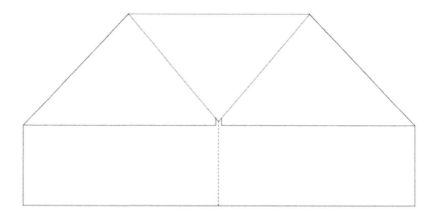

4. Fold down the right edge so that the new vertical edge is aligned with the center crease, as shown in the image below.

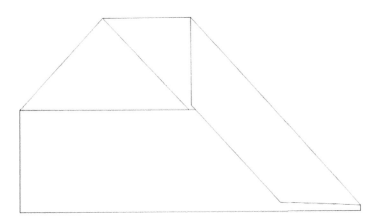

5. Repeat the previous step on the left edge, so that the paper now looks as shown below.

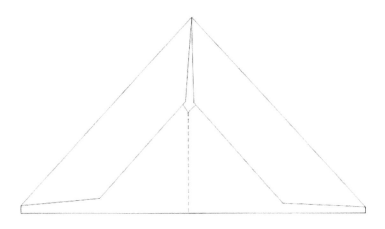

6. Turn your plane over and fold the bottom right corner in until it touches the center crease, as shown below.

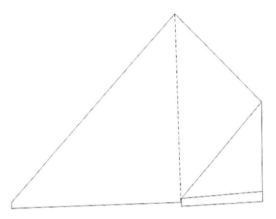

7. Repeat the previous step with the other side so that your plane looks like the image below.

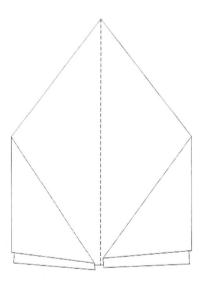

8. Fold the right edge towards the center crease, as shown in the image below.

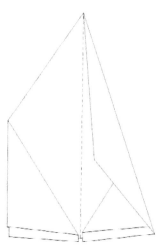

9. Repeat the previous step with the left side so that your plane looks like the image on the next page.

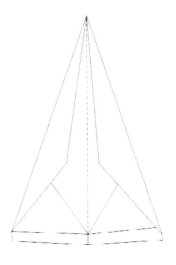

10. Fold your plane in half along the vertical crease so that your paper resembles the image below.

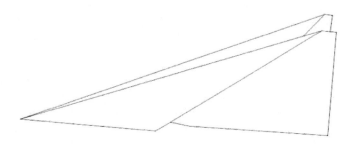

11. Fold down the top flap to form one wing, as shown on the next page.

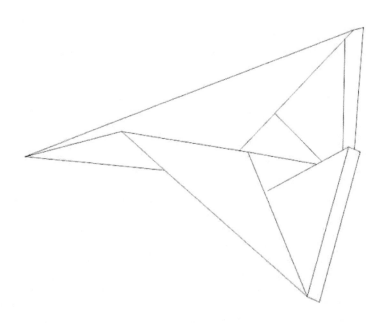

12. Turn your plane over and fold down the other flap to form the second wing.

13. Finally, fold the ends of each wing flap upwards, as shown in the image below.

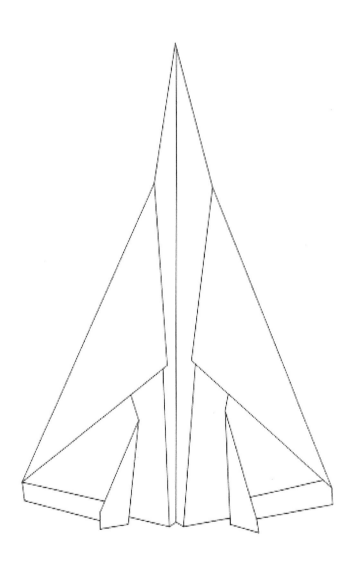

14. Your complete Navy Plane should look like the image below.

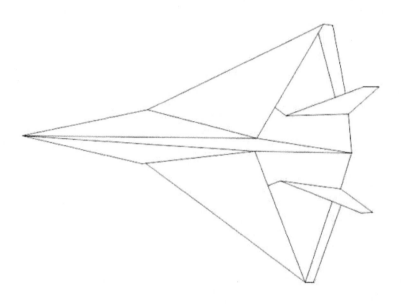

Chapter Five: Expert Level Paper Airplane Designs

In this chapter, we are going to look at expert level paper airplane designs. The planes covered in this section have very complex designs, and will take several minutes to build. However, the planes you will build in this section look very cool. The designs covered in this section are a great way to leave your friends gazing at you in wonder and amazement, since they show that you are an expert in building paper airplanes. In this section, you will also get your first encounter with designs that include the accordion fold, which might seem a bit complex. However, don't let that scare you. You should get the hang of it after the first few tries. Just keep practicing!

Space Shuttle

Like the name suggests, this paper airplane is modeled after the NASA space shuttle. Like any aircraft built for space travel, the space shuttle paper airplane is built for distance rather than speed. It's long, wide wings help it glide perfectly. When launching it into flight, remember to throw it gently.

Folding Instructions

1. Place a rectangular piece of paper with the longest edges on top and bottom and then fold it by half vertically, as shown below.

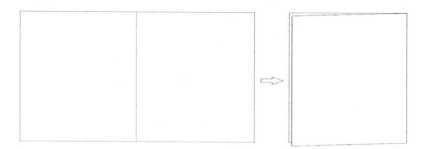

2. Fold the bottom corner of the plane diagonally as shown on the next page, then unfold to create a crease. Flip the paper over and repeat the folding and unfolding process so that the paper is creased on both sides.

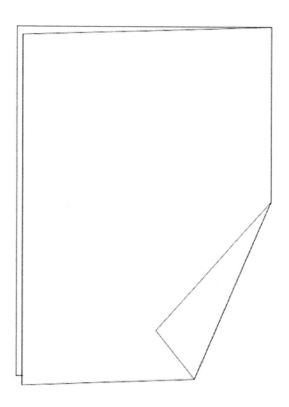

3. Accordion fold the small triangle between the two main flaps, as shown on the next page.

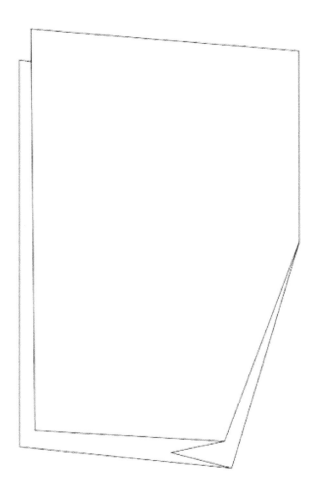

4. Fold the top flap across an imaginary diagonal line running from the top right corner to the bottom left corner. Flip the paper over and fold the other flap the same way so that your paper looks like the image on the next page.

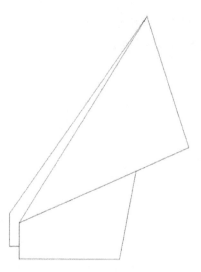

5. Fold the pieces of paper extending over the edge inwards on themselves so that the paper now looks like the image below.

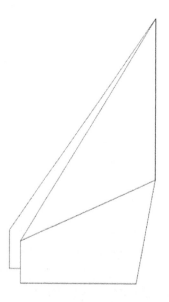

6. Rotate your plane so that the sharp corner points towards your left, then fold down the top flap about half an inch from the bottom edge of the plane. Repeat this with the other flap. Your plane should now resemble the image below.

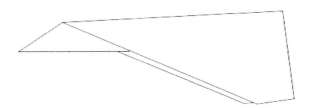

7. Fold the top flap upwards so that its bottom edge aligns with the bottom edge of the plane's body, as shown below.

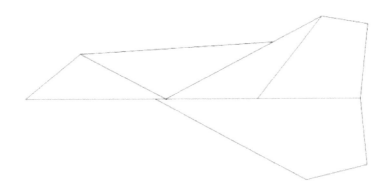

8. Repeat the same process with the bottom flap. Then, open the wings to complete your plane. Your space shuttle should now look like the image on the next page.

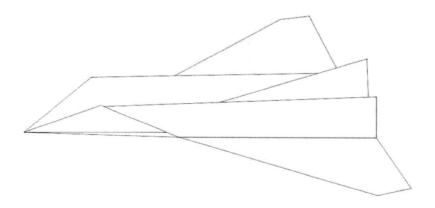

Cross Wing

The Cross Wing is a small plane that is built for speed and distance. When launched hard enough, it will achieve very high speeds and fly for long distances, owing to its small size and heavy nose.

Folding Instructions

1. Fold a piece of paper in half horizontally, as shown below.

2. Fold the paper so that the two top corners do not quite meet in the center of the paper, as shown on the next page.

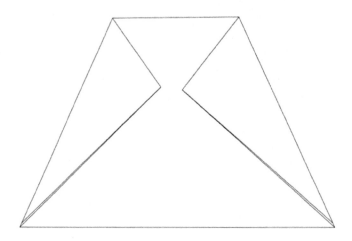

3. Open up the folds you made in the previous step and accordion fold them inwards as shown below.

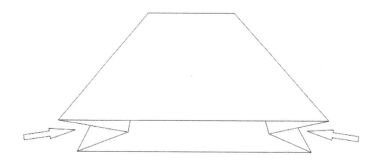

4. After completing Step 3, your paper should now look like the image below.

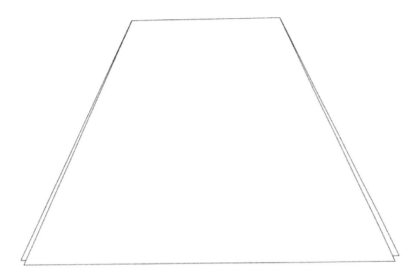

5. Fold down the two top corners so that they meet at the center, as shown below.

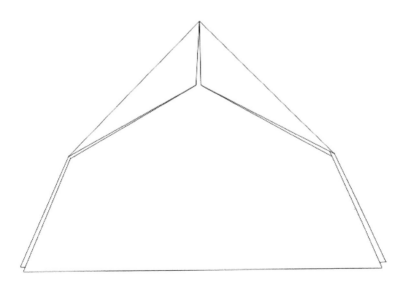

6. About an inch from the top, fold the point down and back, as shown below.

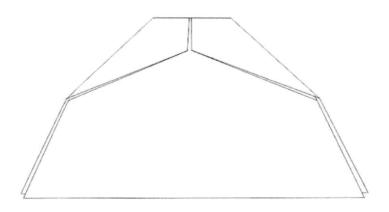

7. Fold the plane in half vertically. Your plane should now look like the image below.

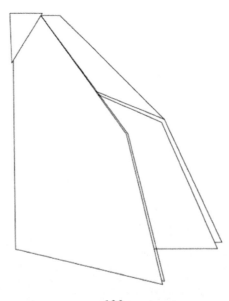

8. Fold the side flaps to form wings for your plane. Fold the edges of the wings upwards about an inch from the tips of the wings. The complete plane should look like the image below.

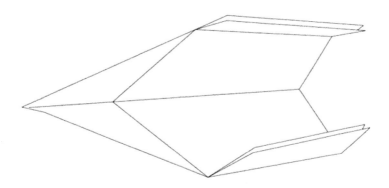

The Square Plane

This is a plane that is designed to fly over long distances, since its boxy shape makes it possible for the plane to glide effortlessly through the air.

Folding Instructions

1. Fold a piece of paper horizontally, leaving about 2 inches of space at the bottom, as shown below.

2. Fold down the two top corners so that they meet at the center, as shown on the next page.

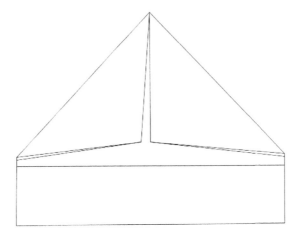

3. Open up the folds you made in the previous step and accordion fold the side flaps as shown below.

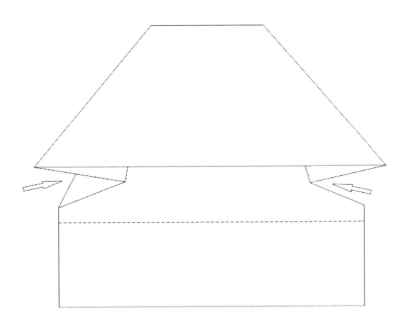

4. After completing step 3, the paper should look like the image below.

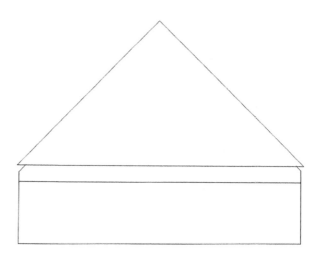

5. Fold the top flap upwards towards the top point, as shown below.

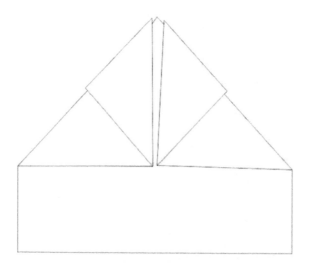

6. Fold down the top point to the center of the paper, as shown below.

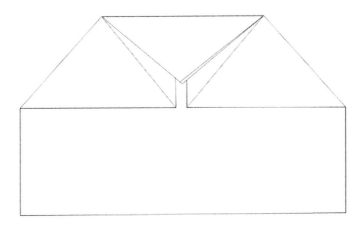

7. Fold the plane in half vertically so that the plane looks like the image below.

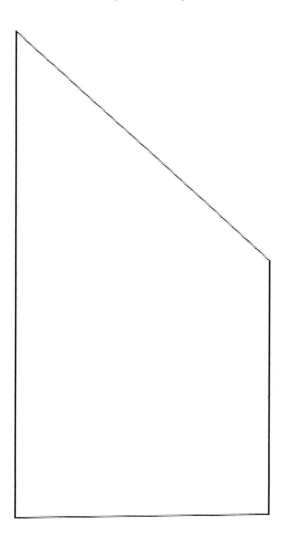

8. Fold out the side flaps to create wings for your plane, as shown below. Make this fold about half an inch from the bottom edge of the plane.

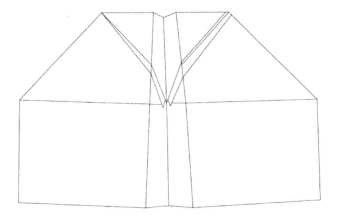

9. Using a pair of scissors, cut two small slits at the tail end of each wing, about half an inch apart. Fold the section of paper between each pair of slits upwards. Your now complete Square Plane should look like the image below.

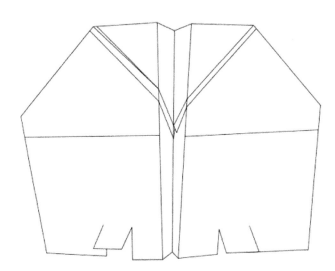

The F-4 Phantom Jet

This paper airplane is modeled after the F-4 Phantom, a supersonic interceptor and fighter bomber which was the main fighter aircraft during the Vietnam War. As you might expect of any fighter bomber, this paper airplane is built for speed.

Folding Instructions

1. Position your paper in landscape mode (longer sides on top and bottom) and then fold it in half vertically. Unfold the paper so that a vertical crease remains, as shown below.

2. Fold the left side of your paper along an imaginary diagonal line running from the top of the centerline crease to the left edge of your paper, as shown below. You should leave about 3 centimeters between the start of the crease and the bottom edge of the paper.

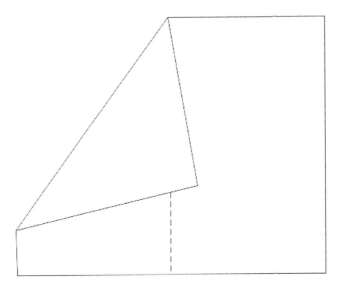

3. Unfold the paper so that a diagonal crease remains. Fold the left edge of your paper so that it aligns with the diagonal crease, as shown below.

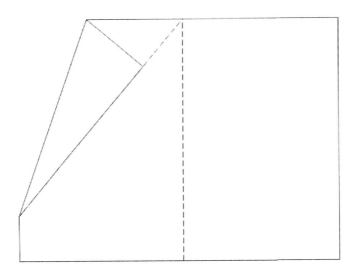

4. Once again, fold the left edge of your paper along the diagonal crease so that your paper now resembles the image shown below.

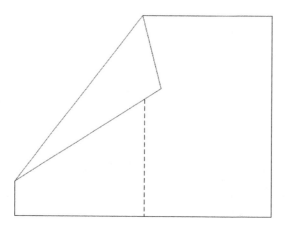

5. Repeat steps 2 through 4 with the right side of your paper so that your paper ends up looking like the image below.

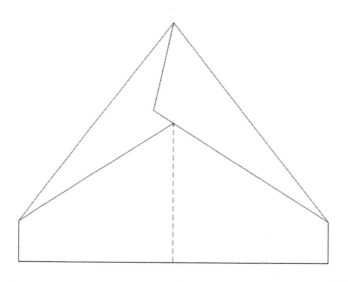

6. Fold your plane in half along the vertical crease so that it looks as shown below.

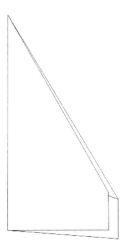

7. Fold the bottom left corner along the diagonal line shown below, then flip your paper over and fold the same point to the other side.

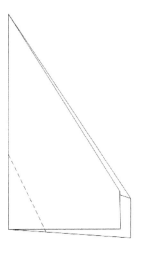

8. Accordion fold this part inwards between the two outer flaps, as shown below.

9. Turn your plane around so that the pointed part faces to your left. Using a ruler, draw the folding lines shown below on your plane.

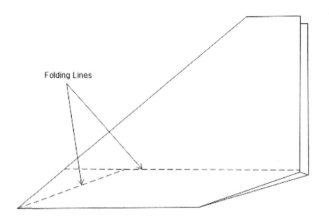

Folding Lines

10. Fold your plane along the lines you just drew, starting with the nose before moving to the body, so that your plane resembles the image below.

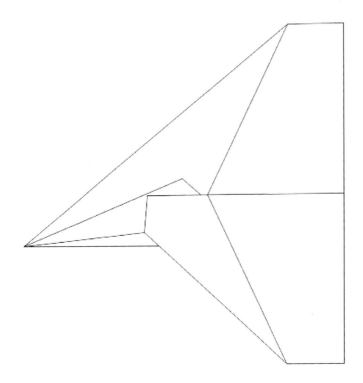

11. Repeat steps 9 through 10 with the other side to create the other wing for your plane. Fold up the side edges of your wings about a centimeter from the tip of the wing.

12. Open one wing and cut it out so that it resembles the image on the next page.

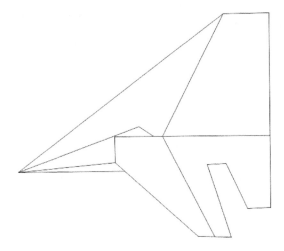

13. Open the other wing and cut it like you did with the first one.

14. Finally, fold down the wings of your plane. Your complete F-4 Phantom jet should look like the image below.

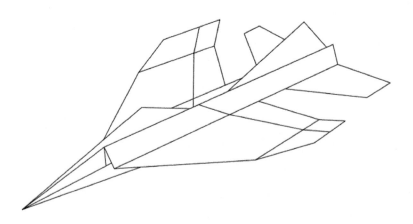

The Star Crusher

The Star Crusher is a sleek paper airplane that will have your friends green with envy. Once you launch this plane into the air, it will amaze you with great acrobatic stunts as it dives and swoops like a fighter jet evading enemy fire. Before you get started, you should note that this is an extremely difficult design. Do not get disheartened if you don't get it right on your first try. Give yourself some time to practice and get comfortable with the complex folds.

Folding Instructions

1. Start by folding a piece of paper by half vertically, and then unfold it so that you are left with a crease along the center, as shown below.

2. Flip the piece of paper over and fold the top left corner till it touches the right edge, as shown on the next page. Ensure that the fold, especially the top right corner is as sharp as possible.

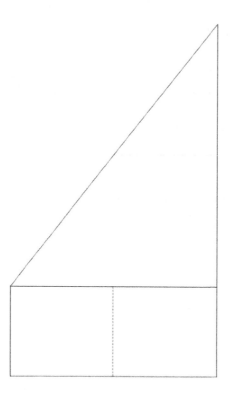

3. Unfold the paper and repeat the previous step, this time folding the top right corner so that it touches the left edge. Make the top left corner as sharp as possible. Then, unfold the paper so that you have three creases, as shown on the next page.

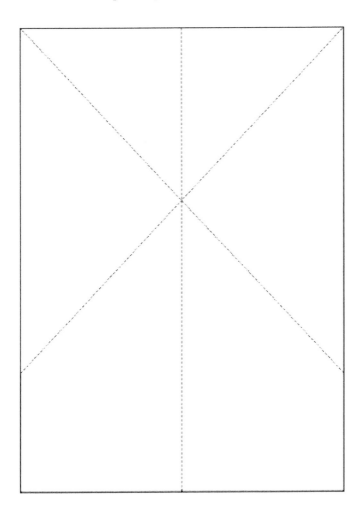

4. Turn the paper over and fold down the top until the corners touch the starting points of the diagonal creases. Unfold so that you have another crease running horizontally, as shown in the image on the next page.

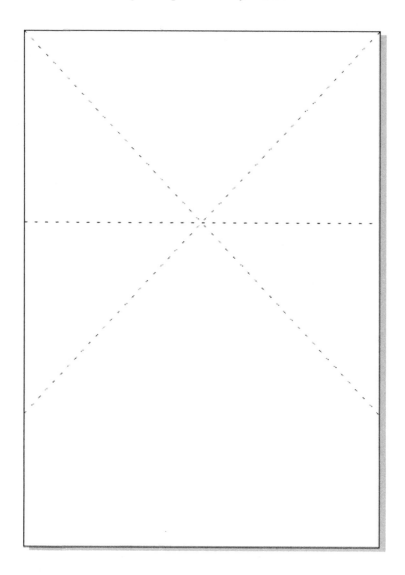

5. Turn the paper over and place your finger at the center where the creases meet to form an "X" shape. Press your finger on this point until the sides of the paper pop up. Your paper should now look as shown on the next page.

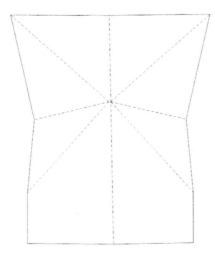

6. Fold the top side of the paper along the horizontal crease and accordion fold the side flaps inwards, as shown below.

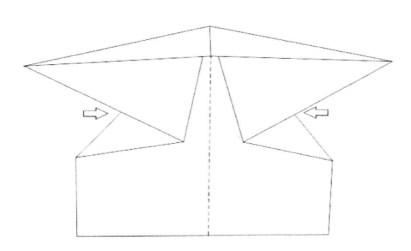

7. Press down the top section until you get the shape shown below.

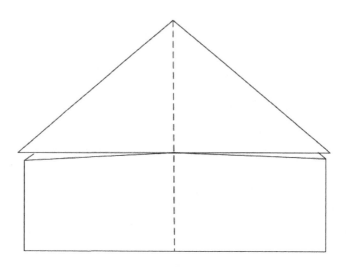

8. Fold the left triangular flap upwards about a thumb's width from the center of the paper, as shown below.

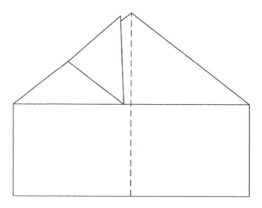

9. Flip the piece of paper over and fold the left side over the right side. Your plane should now resemble the image shown below.

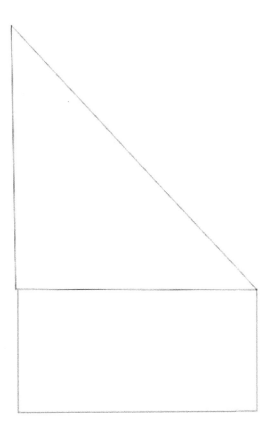

10. Fold the top triangular flap in upwards about a thumb's width from the edge as shown on the next page, taking care to ensure that it aligns well with the other flap on the other side.

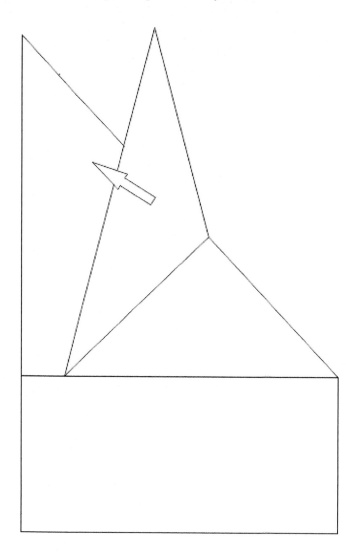

11. After completing step ten, your plane should now look as shown on the next page.

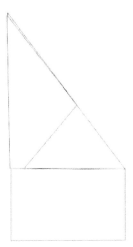

12. Open up the plane so that it looks like the image below.

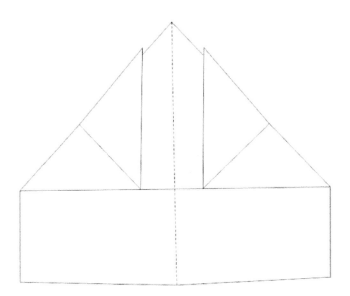

13. Fold the left triangular flap diagonally as shown in the image below and then unfold again so you are left with a crease running diagonally across the flap.

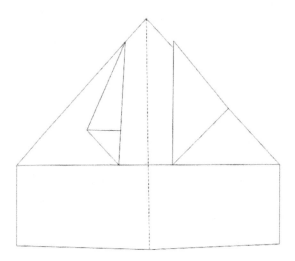

14. Now fold over the left triangular flap so that it covers the right triangular flap.

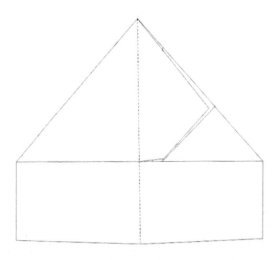

15. Again, fold this flap in half diagonally as shown in the image below. Unfold it so you are left with another crease.

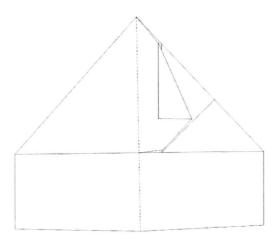

16. Unfold the flap back to the left side where it was originally, and then open it up so that it looks like the image on the next page.

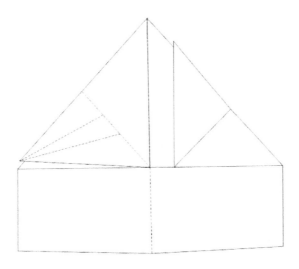

17. Squeeze the flap along the creases you created so that it forms a sharp, fang-like projection, as shown in the image below.

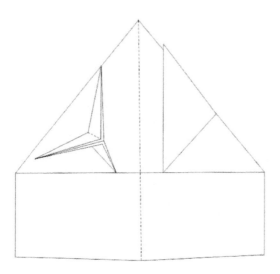

18. Fold the fang-like projection over so that it points upwards.

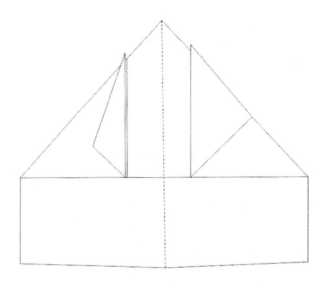

19. Repeat steps 12 – 17 with the right triangular flap. By the end of this step, your plane should look like the image shown below.

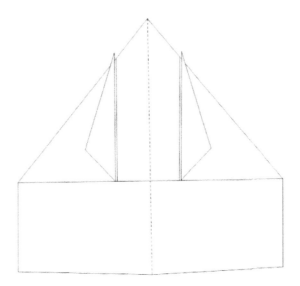

20. Turn your plane over and fold the top point towards the bottom of the plane. Make sure you leave a space. Your plane should now look like the image on the next page.

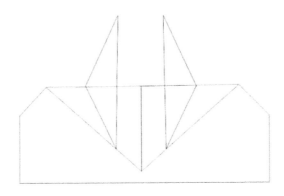

21. Fold the plane in half so that it resembles the image below.

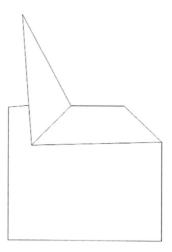

22. With your fingers holding the bottom corner of the fang-like projection, fold the top flap to the left along the crease shown below.

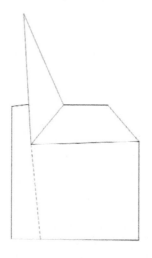

23. Your plane should now look like the image on the next page.

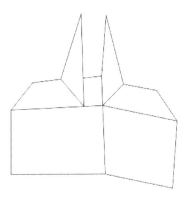

24. Turn the plane over and fold over the other flap so that it aligns with the first wing.

25. Fold the first wing towards the bottom edge of the plane as shown below to create a fin.

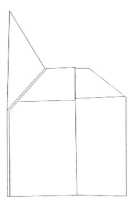

26. Flip the plane over and fold the other wing towards the bottom edge of the plane like you did with the first wing.

27. Finally, open up both wings and fins. The now complete star crusher should look like the image below.

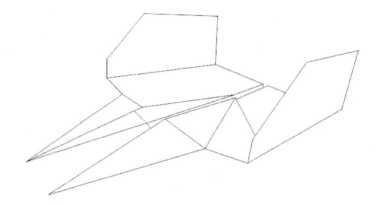

Chapter Six: Tips To Improve The Performance Of Your Paper Airplane

While the ability to turn a piece of paper into a flying machine is exciting, sometimes your paper airplane might not work as you expected. This chapter contains some tips that you can use to improve your paper airplane's flight, making it fly faster, farther, or remain airborne for much longer.

- Shorter wings provide your plane with more lift. If you want your paper airplane to fly higher, fold the wings to make them shorter. Folding the wings can also make the design of your plane more complex, giving your plane a better look. Planes with shorter wings are also more rigid, allowing you to launch the plane faster. While paper airplanes with long, wide wings are good gliders, they need to be launched more gently.

- Always ensure that the wings of your paper airplane are symmetrical. As you make the folds depending on your plane's design, sometimes you might make wrong estimations, leading to one wing being longer or wider than the other. Uneven wings will affect the flight of your plane, making it lean to one side. Therefore, try as much as possible to ensure that the wings are symmetrical. You can do this by unfolding the plane and folding it again or trimming off one wing. However, be careful if you decide to trim, since you cannot undo a mistake when trimming.

- If your plane is nose diving every time, you can correct its flight trajectory by bending the back end of the wings upwards. This moves back your planes center of gravity and gives it stability, allowing it to fly farther and faster.

- If your plane is stalling (going straight up and then crashing back to the ground), you can improve its flight by adding some weight to its nose. This balances the plane and prevents it from flying straight up. You can add weight to the nose either by adding a paper clip or taping a coin to the nose. Heavier planes will handle outdoor conditions better than light planes.

- You can also correct a stalling paper airplane by bending the back ends of the wings downwards. This will prevent the plane from flying upwards after launch.

- If you are having trouble keeping your plane's wings together, you can use double stick tape on the inside of your plane to keep the wings together during flight.

- To avoid your plane coming apart mid-flight, ensure that you have made each fold cleanly and precisely. To make your creases sharp and perfect, you can either run your fingernail or a ruler along the outer edge of the fold.

- The key to your plane's flight lies in its wings. For planes that use a modified version of the dart, you can make their flight faster and smoother by slightly pushing the wings upwards, so that the plane looks like the letter "Y" when observed from the rear, instead of resembling the letter "T."

- You should opt for light to medium thickness paper for your paper airplanes. While some planes work better with heavier paper, it is harder to fold, especially if you are a beginner. Making sharp and accurate creases on heavy paper is hard and sloppy creases can easily ruin your plane's flight.

- For most of the planes discussed in this book, legal A4 or letter-size paper will work perfectly, unless the shape or size of the paper is specified. Even if you do not have access to legal A4 or letter-size paper, you can still make the planes using any rectangular piece of paper.

- Finally, you should be very careful when flying paper airplanes around people, or even by yourself. When properly folded, some of these planes will have a very sharp nose.

Since their flights can be unpredictable, these planes can cause injury, for instance, if they fly into someone's eye. If there are people around you, notify them before you launch your plane into the air.

Final Words

Congratulations!

You have come to the end of this book of great paper airplane designs.

By now, you should have expert-level skills in building paper airplanes. You can step out into the world confidently knowing that none of your friends will be able to compete with your skills. You can also use your skills to impress your friends at school, at parties, or when you are out for picnics. The numerous plane designs provided in this book also mean that you will never run out of new designs to try. Now go out there and show everyone that you're the best pilot in the neighborhood!

If you have enjoyed this book, I would also like to request you leave your honest feedback. Your feedback will be greatly appreciated, and will help me keep producing such great books for you.

Printed in Great Britain
by Amazon

82595263R00092